Warsh_ps

Henry Brook

Designed by Helen Edmonds
and Zoe Wray

Illustrated by Adrian Dean and Adrian Roots
Picture strips by Staz Johnson

Edited by Alex Frith
Warships expert: Stephen Courtney, National Museum of the Royal Navy

Contents

American battleship *USS Iowa* fires a broadside from her main guns during a weapons test in 1984.

What is a warship?

A warship is any water-based craft armed with troops and weapons.

Warships carry out combat missions at sea, patrol coastlines, protect friendly ships and move supplies to distant battle zones.

The oldest known warships date back at least 3,000 years – near the beginning of written history.

Basic parts of a warship

There are many types of modern warships. This one is called a destroyer.

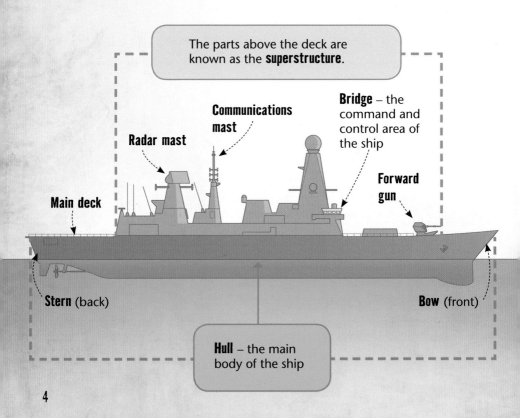

The parts above the deck are known as the **superstructure**.

Communications mast

Radar mast

Bridge – the command and control area of the ship

Forward gun

Main deck

Stern (back)

Bow (front)

Hull – the main body of the ship

Here are some of the main types of warships used today:

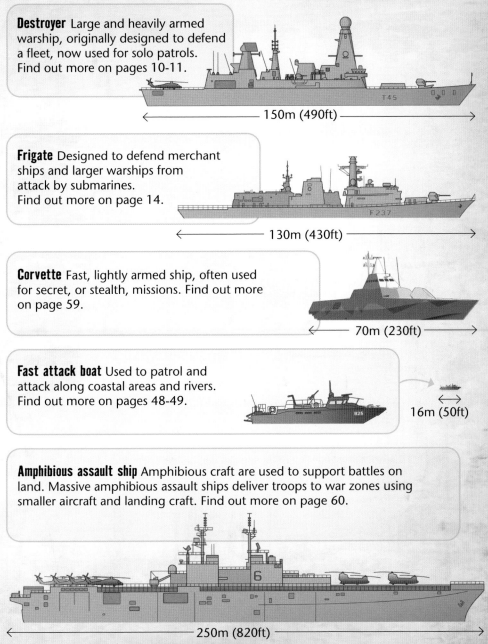

Destroyer Large and heavily armed warship, originally designed to defend a fleet, now used for solo patrols. Find out more on pages 10-11.

150m (490ft)

Frigate Designed to defend merchant ships and larger warships from attack by submarines. Find out more on page 14.

130m (430ft)

Corvette Fast, lightly armed ship, often used for secret, or stealth, missions. Find out more on page 59.

70m (230ft)

Fast attack boat Used to patrol and attack along coastal areas and rivers. Find out more on pages 48-49.

16m (50ft)

Amphibious assault ship Amphibious craft are used to support battles on land. Massive amphibious assault ships deliver troops to war zones using smaller aircraft and landing craft. Find out more on page 60.

250m (820ft)

Meet the fleet

Modern warships often patrol together in an imposing fleet known as a strike group, a battle group or a task force.

Here, the US Navy's *Nassau Strike Group* patrols the Atlantic Ocean. *USS Nassau*, at the heart of the group, is an amphibious assault ship.

This strike group includes a cruiser – an older warship slightly bigger and more powerful than a destroyer.

Landing ship

Destroyer

Cruiser

Amphibious assault ship

The central ship in a strike group is usually an aircraft carrier or amphibious assault ship. These ships carry some of the most important naval weapons: aircraft.

Landing ship

Some groups sail with extra landing ships. These transport troops and heavy war machines directly to war zones on land.

Destroyer

Escorts

Destroyers, cruisers or frigates patrol at the front and back of the group. They defend the group against enemy aircraft and ships.

Ready for battle

The main weapons on modern warships are rocket-powered missiles. They can destroy incoming planes and missiles, strike enemy ships and blast land targets hundreds of miles away.

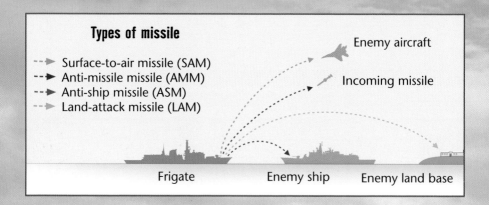

Types of missile

- - -▶ Surface-to-air missile (SAM)
- - ▶ Anti-missile missile (AMM)
- - ▶ Anti-ship missile (ASM)
- - ▶ Land-attack missile (LAM)

Enemy aircraft

Incoming missile

Frigate   Enemy ship   Enemy land base

Vertical launch

Missiles are usually fired using a Vertical Launch System. They shoot up from bays hidden under the main deck.

Most big warships carry a forward gun and two central short-range guns. Find out more on pages 10a-11a.

70

The captain

The commander of a warship is known as the captain, although captains often hold a rank with a different title.

The captain moves from commanding the ship on the bridge to watching over combat missions in the operations room.

On the bridge

❶ **Officer of the Watch** – to keep the ship on course

❷ **Helmsman** – to steer the ship

❸ **Lookout** – to watch for enemy vessels, and signals from friendly vessels

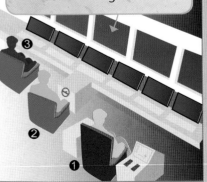

Windows looking out to sea

The captain, on the left, is looking at a situation display screen. This shows the location of any nearby ships, aircraft and incoming missiles.

Type 45 destroyer

New warships are often described by their group or class. The latest British destroyer is known as the Type 45.

Here is a model of the ship. Parts have been cut away so you can see inside.

The first Type 45 built was called *HMS Daring*. Type 45s are also known as the Daring class.

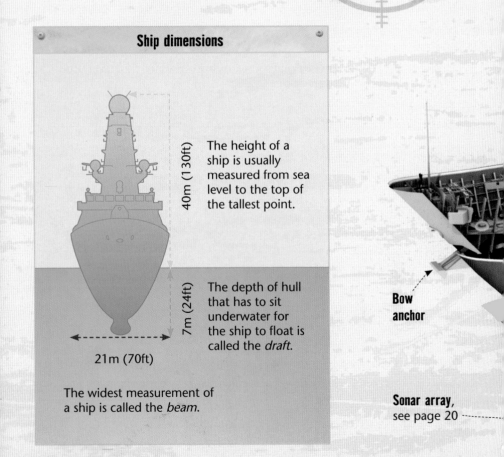

Ship dimensions

40m (130ft)

The height of a ship is usually measured from sea level to the top of the tallest point.

7m (24ft)

The depth of hull that has to sit underwater for the ship to float is called the *draft*.

21m (70ft)

The widest measurement of a ship is called the *beam*.

Bow anchor

Sonar array,
see page 20

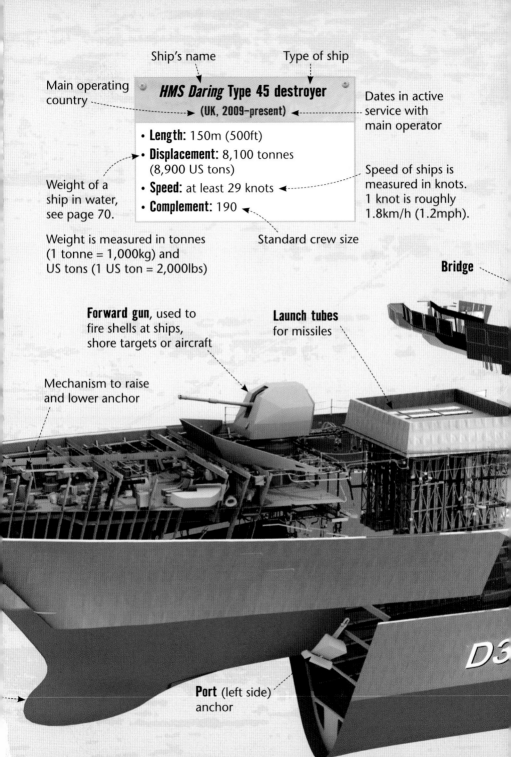

Ship's name

Type of ship

Main operating country

HMS Daring Type 45 destroyer
(UK, 2009–present)

Dates in active service with main operator

- **Length:** 150m (500ft)
- **Displacement:** 8,100 tonnes (8,900 US tons)
- **Speed:** at least 29 knots
- **Complement:** 190

Weight of a ship in water, see page 70.

Weight is measured in tonnes (1 tonne = 1,000kg) and US tons (1 US ton = 2,000lbs)

Standard crew size

Speed of ships is measured in knots. 1 knot is roughly 1.8km/h (1.2mph).

Bridge

Forward gun, used to fire shells at ships, shore targets or aircraft

Launch tubes for missiles

Mechanism to raise and lower anchor

D3

Port (left side) anchor

This American destroyer has just launched an SM3 anti-missile missile as part of a test.

Radar mast. Radar operators on board ensure the missile stays on target after it has been fired.

Officers and ratings

A crew is made up of ratings – sailors who carry out different jobs onboard – and their officers, who control the running of the ship.

A fleet commander inspects the crew of *USS Nassau*, an amphibious assault ship. The full crew numbers 82 officers and 882 ratings.

Radar antenna, see pages 56-57

Communications mast

Operations room

Ventilation system, for exhaust gases from the engines

Officers' cabins

Fuel tanks in here

Galley – kitchen and eating area

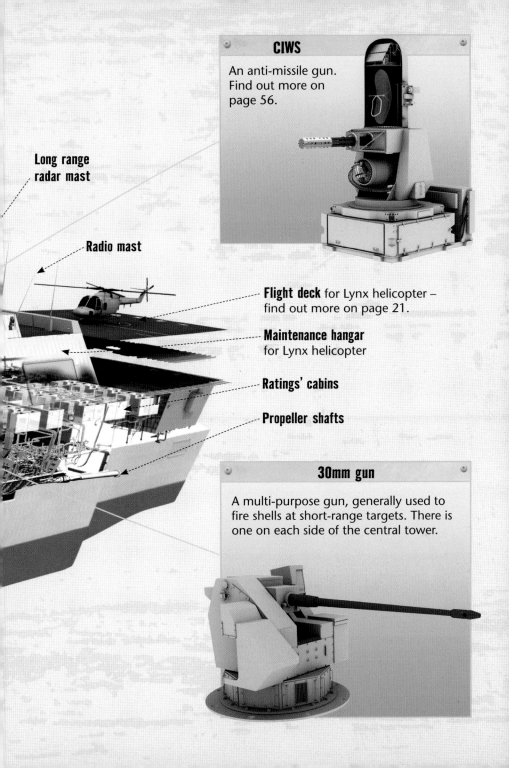

CIWS

An anti-missile gun. Find out more on page 56.

Long range radar mast

Radio mast

Flight deck for Lynx helicopter – find out more on page 21.

Maintenance hangar for Lynx helicopter

Ratings' cabins

Propeller shafts

30mm gun

A multi-purpose gun, generally used to fire shells at short-range targets. There is one on each side of the central tower.

This is the operations room on a Type 42 destroyer. The crew members are wearing flame-proof flash suits as part of a combat exercise.

In the operations room

1. **Captain or warfare officer** – who decides which targets to fire at
2. **Fire control officers** – who activate the missiles and torpedoes
3. **Situation display area**
4. **Radar operators**
5. **Sonar operators**
6. **Communications hub**

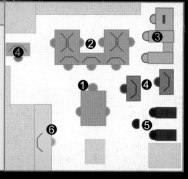

Life on board a destroyer

A destroyer needs a crew of around 200 sailors, operators and engineers. Everyone on board is vital to the security and combat readiness of the ship.

Galley

Operations room

Machinery space

Bridge

Flight deck and hangar

Missile silo and launch tubes

Forward gun

Weapons engineer: maintains the guns and missile launchers.

Operators and technicians: different teams repair the engines and oversee the computer systems.

Helicopter engineer: checks the helicopters and prepares them for take-off.

Head chef: works in the galley and oversees preparation of three meals a day for the entire crew.

A ship for any mission

Warships are built to handle a range of tasks and missions. Some cross oceans to launch attacks, others operate in the littoral (coastal) zone, close to shore.

A Type 23 frigate. These warships were designed to hunt submarines, but developed into multi-purpose fighting ships.

Type 23 frigate
(UK, 1987–present)

- **Length:** 130m (440ft)
- **Displacement:** 4,900 tonnes (5,400 US tons)
- **Max. speed:** 34 knots
- **Complement:** 185

Read a story about a Type 23 in action on pages 16-17.

Amphibious ships aren't only used to support missions on land. In 2008, French Mistral class ship *Tonerre* helped to raid two drug-smuggling vessels.

Mistral class amphibious assault ship
(France, 2009–present)

- **Length:** 200m (650ft)
- **Displacement:** 32,300 tonnes (35,600 US tons)
- **Max. speed:** 19 knots
- **Complement:** 160 crew + 900 troops

USS *Independence* littoral combat ship
(USA, 2011–present)

- **Length:** 127m (418ft)
- **Displacement:** 2,400 tonnes (2,700 US tons)
- **Max. speed:** 44 knots
- **Complement:** 75

Speedy littoral combat ships are used to protect borders and fight piracy.

Zubr class landing craft
(Russia, 1988–present)

- **Length:** 57m (187ft)
- **Displacement:** 550 tonnes (600 US tons)
- **Max. speed:** 63 knots
- **Complement:** 31

Landing craft take troops and vehicles onto beaches. The Zubr's air cushion floats on water and allows it to climb walls up to 1.6m (5ft, 6in) high.

Pirate patrol

Since the end of the Second World War, combat at sea has been rare. But modern warships are ready to cope with surprises. This story shows how a Royal Navy frigate might respond to a pirate incident.

A British Type 23 frigate is on patrol in the Indian Ocean. The radio operator picks up a distress call...

...S.O.S. This is yacht 'Sally'. We are under attack by pirates. The captain has already been taken hostage. Location is...

The radio operator finds the yacht's location, and the captain orders the ship to get there at maximum speed.

The captain then orders the radar operators to scan for signs of a possible pirate ship in the area...

...and sends a helicopter crew into the air to investigate.

The pirates are tracked to a base on a nearby island. An assault team of marine commandos leaves the frigate on a fast attack boat.

From the bridge of the frigate, the captain is in radio contact with the helicopter pilot and the assault team.

The captain gives the order to open fire, and a gunner in the operations room fires a salvo of shells from the forward gun. These destroy weapons positions around the pirates' base.

Under the cover of fire and smoke, the assault team rushes in and arrests the pirates. The commandos lead the hostages out to safety.

A floating airbase

The most powerful ship in any modern navy is the aircraft carrier. The biggest carry 90 helicopters and fighter planes.

A squadron of Super Hornet fighter planes prepares to launch from the *USS Dwight D. Eisenhower*.

The wings on these fighter planes can fold up, so they take up less space on the ship.

A catapult on the track helps launch the planes.

USS Dwight D. Eisenhower is a Nimitz class ship. They're so big they're known as supercarriers.

An elevator platform brings planes up from the hangar deck below.

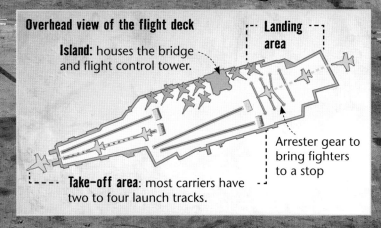

Overhead view of the flight deck

Island: houses the bridge and flight control tower.

Landing area

Arrester gear to bring fighters to a stop

Take-off area: most carriers have two to four launch tracks.

Air support

Most warships larger than a corvette carry at least one helicopter. These are used to hunt for submarines, carry elite troops to war zones, and lead search and rescue missions.

Sub hunting

Warships listen for submarines using a technique known as sonar, or send out helicopters to spot them. Some helicopters use a technique called magnetic anomaly detection to search for subs.

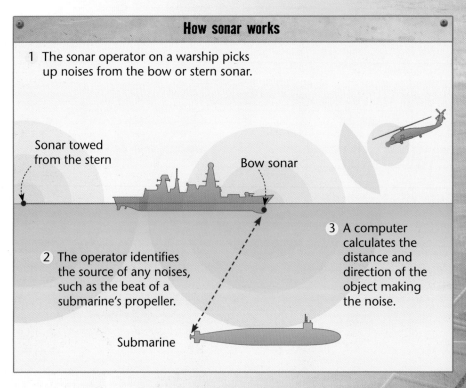

How sonar works

1 The sonar operator on a warship picks up noises from the bow or stern sonar.

Sonar towed from the stern

Bow sonar

3 A computer calculates the distance and direction of the object making the noise.

2 The operator identifies the source of any noises, such as the beat of a submarine's propeller.

Submarine

A Super Lynx helicopter taking off from the deck of a frigate

Westland Super Lynx
(UK, 1983–present)

- **Length:** 15m (50ft)
- **Range:** 530km (330 miles)
- **Max. speed:** 325km/h (200mph)
- **Crew:** 2 or 3 + 10 troops

The helicopter is armed with machine guns, and carries either missiles or anti-submarine torpedoes.

Early fighting ships

Warships have been used for thousands of years. The first had sails for long voyages, but for speed and control in battle, naval commanders used galleys – ships powered by rows of oarsmen.

Ramming speed

A galley's main weapon was an underwater ram at the bow. Oarsmen powered the ship through the water so they could smash the ram into enemy hulls.

Trireme galley
(Ancient Greece, about 2,500 years ago)

Triremes had three rows of oars, each oar pulled by one oarsman – often a slave.

Metal plated ram

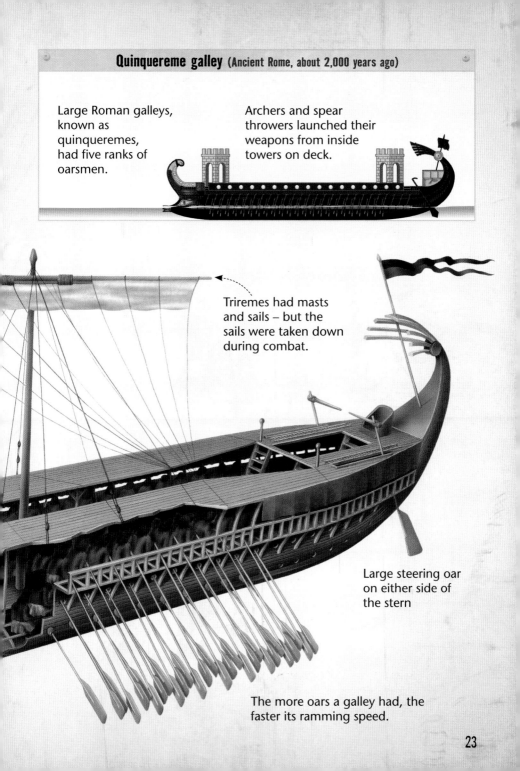

Quinquereme galley (Ancient Rome, about 2,000 years ago)

Large Roman galleys, known as quinqueremes, had five ranks of oarsmen.

Archers and spear throwers launched their weapons from inside towers on deck.

Triremes had masts and sails – but the sails were taken down during combat.

Large steering oar on either side of the stern

The more oars a galley had, the faster its ramming speed.

Sails and guns

Triremes were fast, but they couldn't fight in the open sea.
Navies needed warships with broad hulls and wide sails,
that could make longer voyages and, later, carry heavy guns.

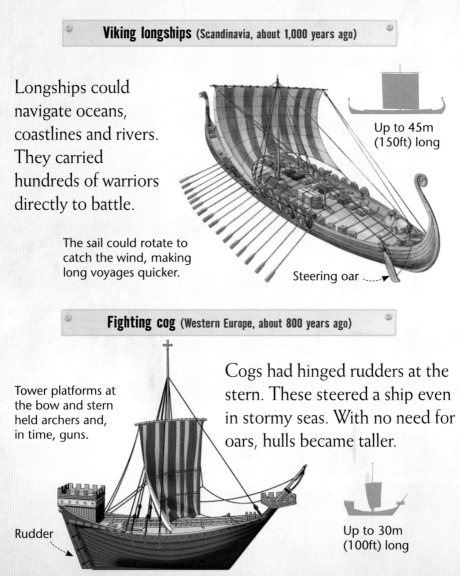

Viking longships (Scandinavia, about 1,000 years ago)

Longships could navigate oceans, coastlines and rivers. They carried hundreds of warriors directly to battle.

Up to 45m (150ft) long

The sail could rotate to catch the wind, making long voyages quicker.

Steering oar

Fighting cog (Western Europe, about 800 years ago)

Tower platforms at the bow and stern held archers and, in time, guns.

Cogs had hinged rudders at the stern. These steered a ship even in stormy seas. With no need for oars, hulls became taller.

Rudder

Up to 30m (100ft) long

Galleons used several sets of sails, which gave them great speed and agility. Huge hulls carried rows and rows of guns.

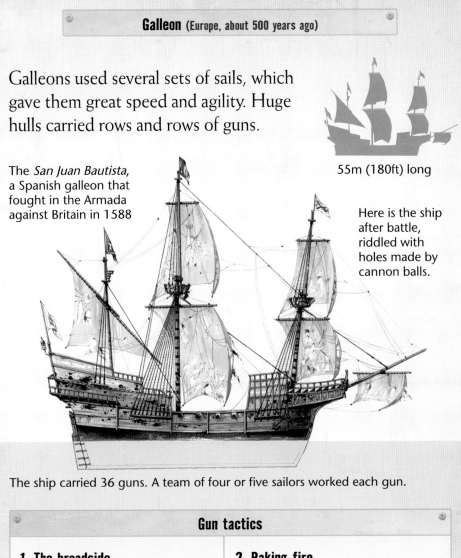

55m (180ft) long

The *San Juan Bautista*, a Spanish galleon that fought in the Armada against Britain in 1588

Here is the ship after battle, riddled with holes made by cannon balls.

The ship carried 36 guns. A team of four or five sailors worked each gun.

Gun tactics

1. The broadside

Every gun on one side of the ship fires together at the *side* of an enemy warship.

2. Raking fire

The guns are pointed at the *stern* or *bow* of an enemy ship, so the shots pass along its length.

The golden age of sail

Sailing ships dominated warfare at sea until the mid-19th century. One of the finest warships of this golden age was *HMS Victory*.

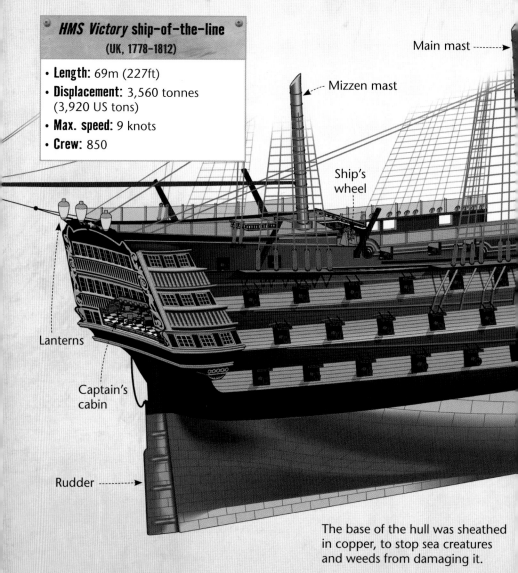

HMS Victory ship-of-the-line
(UK, 1778–1812)

- **Length:** 69m (227ft)
- **Displacement:** 3,560 tonnes (3,920 US tons)
- **Max. speed:** 9 knots
- **Crew:** 850

Main mast

Mizzen mast

Ship's wheel

Lanterns

Captain's cabin

Rudder

The base of the hull was sheathed in copper, to stop sea creatures and weeds from damaging it.

Line of death

HMS Victory was classed as a *ship-of-the-line* – a warship designed to be part of a long line of ships that could fire deadly broadsides while withstanding enemy fire.

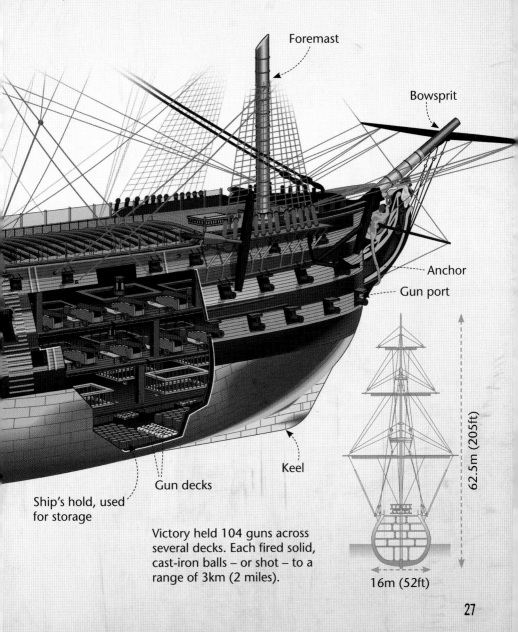

Foremast

Bowsprit

Anchor

Gun port

Keel

Gun decks

Ship's hold, used for storage

Victory held 104 guns across several decks. Each fired solid, cast-iron balls – or shot – to a range of 3km (2 miles).

62.5m (205ft)

16m (52ft)

Nelson's victory

In 1805, war raged across Europe. The French emperor, Napoleon Bonaparte, had conquered Spain and planned to invade Britain.

Horatio Nelson, an admiral of the British Royal Navy, chased Napoleon's fleet around the Mediterranean Sea and Atlantic Ocean for months.

Finally, the two fleets clashed in the greatest sea battle of the age of sail – the Battle of Trafalgar...

Napoleon's fleet of French and Spanish warships sailed out of Cadiz, on the southwest coast of Spain. His ships were drawn up in lines, so their gunners could fire broadsides at attackers.

HMS Victory – Nelson's ship

SPAIN

Cadiz

Cape Trafalgar

British fleet: 27 ships

French and Spanish fleet: 33 ships

Nelson, an aggressive commander, was ready to take a big risk. He decided to sail directly at the enemy line in two long columns. He wanted to break the line and move in for a close-combat trial of gunnery skills.

Nelson's ship, *HMS Victory*, rammed through the enemy line and raked the ships on either side.

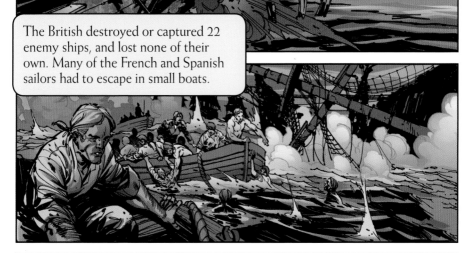

The British destroyed or captured 22 enemy ships, and lost none of their own. Many of the French and Spanish sailors had to escape in small boats.

Napoleon's gun crews were no match for the British sailors, and Nelson's daring won him the battle.

But he never fought again. Nelson was shot by a sniper and only lived long enough to be sure of a British victory.

Ironclads

In the 1850s, warship guns started firing hollow shells filled with explosives to blast wooden ships. Shipbuilders responded by bolting heavy iron plates onto wooden hulls. This created a new breed of warships, known as ironclads.

Funnel to vent exhaust gasses from the engine

Turret rotated to fire in all directions

Propeller at the stern

USS Monitor ironclad
(US, Feb. 1862–Dec. 1862)

- **Length:** 50m (170ft)
- **Displacement:** 1,000 tonnes (1,100 US tons)
- **Max. speed:** 8 knots
- **Complement:** 59

US Navy officials inspect dents in the gun turret of the *Monitor*. The ship had exchanged fire with an enemy ironclad, but neither ship sank.

A floating fortress

By the 1890s, tough steel replaced iron and wood. New, heavily protected warships carried two guns in turrets at the bow and stern. They became known as battleships.

Battleship protection

Battleships used coal- and steam-powered engines, hidden deep in the hull to protect against potentially enormous explosions from enemy shells.

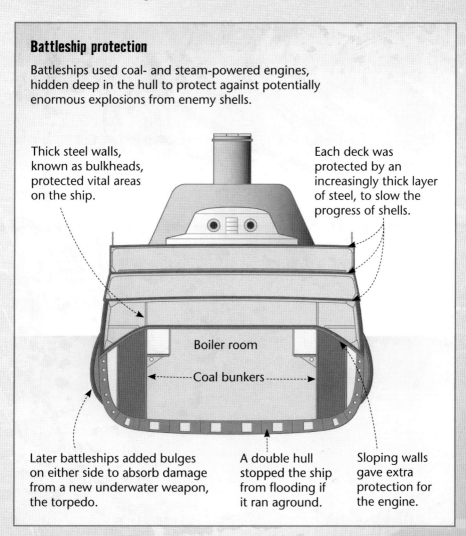

Thick steel walls, known as bulkheads, protected vital areas on the ship.

Each deck was protected by an increasingly thick layer of steel, to slow the progress of shells.

Boiler room

Coal bunkers

Later battleships added bulges on either side to absorb damage from a new underwater weapon, the torpedo.

A double hull stopped the ship from flooding if it ran aground.

Sloping walls gave extra protection for the engine.

Dreadnoughts

In 1906, the British Royal Navy launched a battleship that was faster and tougher than anything else afloat – *HMS Dreadnought*, meaning 'fear nothing'. Soon, a new generation of battleships was built to the same design. They were known as dreadnoughts.

HMS Dreadnought battleship
(UK 1907–1919)

- **Length:** 160m (530ft)
- **Displacement:** 21,000 tonnes (23,200 US tons)
- **Max. speed:** 21 knots
- **Complement:** 810

Guns and nets

Dreadnought had ten big guns across five turrets – twice as many as any other warship at the time.

Anti-torpedo net, raised when the ship was at anchor

Members of the public rowed out to sea to watch King Edward VII launch *HMS Dreadnought* in 1906.

Firing the guns

Dreadnoughts and battleships often had as many as 50 gunners to load, aim and fire each gun. The shells used could each weigh as much as a small car.

Inside a turret

A fire control team calculated wind speed, distance, surface speed and direction of a target, then passed the information to the gun crew, who worked inside each gun turret.

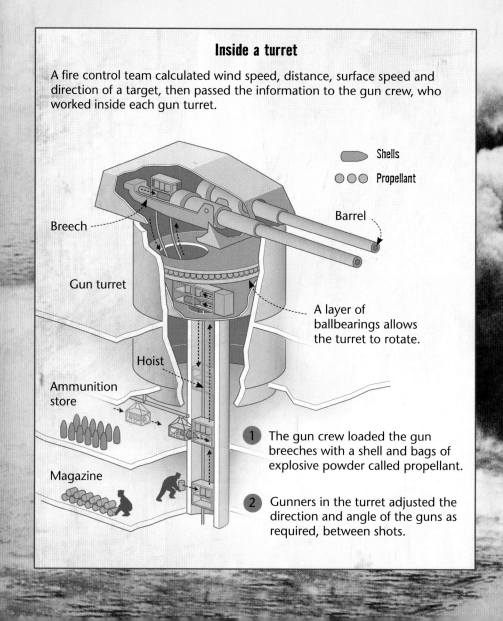

Shells

Propellant

Barrel

Breech

Gun turret

A layer of ballbearings allows the turret to rotate.

Hoist

Ammunition store

Magazine

1 The gun crew loaded the gun breeches with a shell and bags of explosive powder called propellant.

2 Gunners in the turret adjusted the direction and angle of the guns as required, between shots.

Early computers, called Dreyer fire control tables, helped calculate how to aim the guns.

Gunners on the American battleship *USS New Hampshire* fire a broadside as part of a training exercise in 1918.

Turrets

35

The First World War

Britain and Germany began building dreadnoughts and bigger, heavily-gunned super-dreadnoughts. Both countries expected a decisive clash. It came in the sea battles of the First World War, which broke out in 1914.

König class battleship (Germany, 1914–1919)

- **Length:** 175m (575ft)
- **Displacement:** 29,100 tonnes (32,000 US tons)
- **Max. speed:** 21 knots
- **Complement:** 1,136

SMS *Kronprinz*, a König class ship that fought at the Battle of Jutland (see pages 38-39)

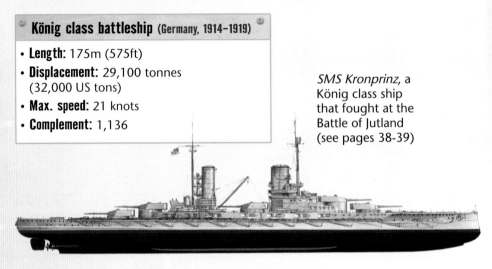

Revenge class battleship (UK, 1916–1939)

- **Length:** 190m (620ft)
- **Displacement:** 33,500 tonnes (36,900 US tons)
- **Max. speed:** 20 knots
- **Complement:** 1,000

HMS *Royal Oak*, a Revenge class ship that also fought at Jutland. It was sunk by a submarine in the Second World War.

Type U31 submarine (Germany, 1914–1918)

- **Length:** 64m (210ft)
- **Displacement:** 970 tonnes (1,070 US tons)
- **Max. speed:** 17 knots (surfaced); 10 knots (submerged)
- **Complement:** 35

The first submarine fleets were built at the start of the 20th century.

Early subs spent most of their time on the surface. They dived to hide from enemy ships.

HMS Killour, a gunboat used to bombard coastal targets, sporting dazzle camouflage

Dazzle ships

In 1916, the British Royal Navy tried painting some of its warships with a pattern known as dazzle camouflage. This didn't hide a ship, but made it difficult for enemies to judge its speed and course.

By the end of the Second World War, dazzle was abandoned as it made the ships easier targets for bomber planes.

Boy hero at Jutland

It was the Summer of 1916, at the height of the First World War, and the world's most powerful navies were about to clash at the Battle of Jutland...

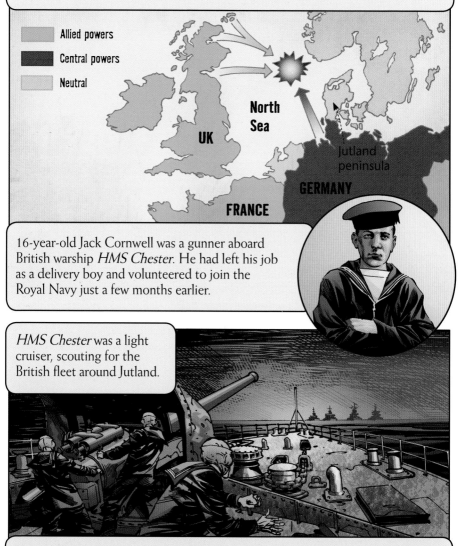

Allied powers

Central powers

Neutral

North Sea

UK

Jutland peninsula

GERMANY

FRANCE

16-year-old Jack Cornwell was a gunner aboard British warship *HMS Chester*. He had left his job as a delivery boy and volunteered to join the Royal Navy just a few months earlier.

HMS Chester was a light cruiser, scouting for the British fleet around Jutland.

Jack was one of the gunners assigned to the ship's forward gun. Among drifting smoke, Jack and the crew of the *Chester* sighted four German cruisers, closing in to attack.

Heavy shells from the German ships exploded on the deck of the *Chester*. After the first volley, Jack was the only forward gunner still alive.

Jack was badly wounded, but he stayed by the gun, waiting for orders.

Eventually, the *Chester* managed to escape. Crews on the British fleet cheered the brave survivors as the ship made its way back to England.

The British fleet suffered heavy losses, but held its position until the end of the battle. Both sides claimed victory.

Jack died of his wounds soon after. He was awarded the Victoria Cross medal for his courage under fire, and received a hero's funeral.

The Second World War

Ships of all sizes fought in the global conflict of 1939-1945, from giant aircraft carriers to stalking submarines.

This picture shows parts of the interior of the *USS Enterprise*.

Machine guns were positioned all along the gallery deck, just below the hangar level.

The *Enterprise* carried up to 80 aircraft. Catapults on the flight deck could launch two aircraft in quick succession.

During the War, 77 Gato class submarines destroyed hundreds of enemy ships – mostly in the Pacific Ocean.

Gato class submarine (USA, 1943-1969)

- **Length:** up to 95m (311ft)
- **Displacement:** 2,500 tonnes (2,700 US tons)
- **Max. speed:** 21 knots surfaced; 9 knots submerged
- **Complement:** 60

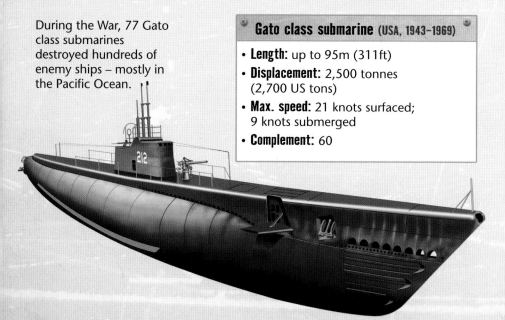

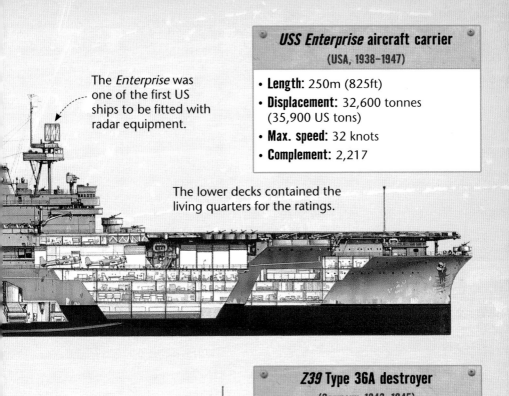

USS *Enterprise* aircraft carrier
(USA, 1938–1947)

The *Enterprise* was one of the first US ships to be fitted with radar equipment.

- **Length:** 250m (825ft)
- **Displacement:** 32,600 tonnes (35,900 US tons)
- **Max. speed:** 32 knots
- **Complement:** 2,217

The lower decks contained the living quarters for the ratings.

Z39 Type 36A destroyer
(Germany, 1943–1945)

The *Z39* had a huge twin gun turret at the front, giving it more firepower than most destroyers.

- **Length:** 125m (410ft)
- **Displacement:** 3,800 tonnes (4,100 US tons)
- **Max. speed:** 37 knots
- **Complement:** 220

After the war, *Z39* was taken over by the US Navy.

Raiders and convoys

Throughout the War, British supply ships carrying weapons and food faced a hazardous voyage. The threat came from attacks by German submarines, known as U-boats, and deadly warships.

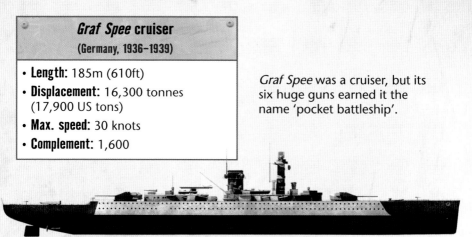

Graf Spee cruiser
(Germany, 1936–1939)

- **Length:** 185m (610ft)
- **Displacement:** 16,300 tonnes (17,900 US tons)
- **Max. speed:** 30 knots
- **Complement:** 1,600

Graf Spee was a cruiser, but its six huge guns earned it the name 'pocket battleship'.

Graf Spee terrorized British shipping lanes during the first months of the War, until British cruisers caught up with her in December 1939.

After a brutal exchange of shells near the river Plate, the *Graf Spee* ran to Montevideo. The captain sank the ship a few days later.

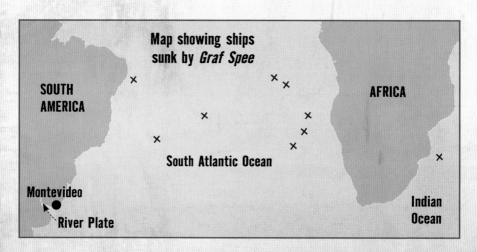

Map showing ships sunk by *Graf Spee*

SOUTH AMERICA

AFRICA

South Atlantic Ocean

Montevideo

River Plate

Indian Ocean

Safety in numbers

In time, the Royal Navy learned they could scare off German raiders if their ships sailed in large convoys, protected by fast warships acting as escorts.

The whole convoy sailed in a zigzag course.

German U-boats hunted convoys in groups known as wolfpacks. But they had to use radio signals to stay in touch, giving away their position.

A **corvette** guarded the rear.

Supply ships sailed together in the middle, all at the same speed.

Destroyers protected the convoy from the side, sailing back and forth to scare off lurking U-boats.

A **cruiser** at the front scouted for enemy ships using radar.

Battle of the battleships

In May 1941, two great battleships clashed in the Atlantic Ocean. *HMS Hood* was the pride of the British fleet, but it was facing one of the most powerful battleships of the day – *Bismarck*.

Until 1940, *HMS Hood* was the biggest battleship at sea.

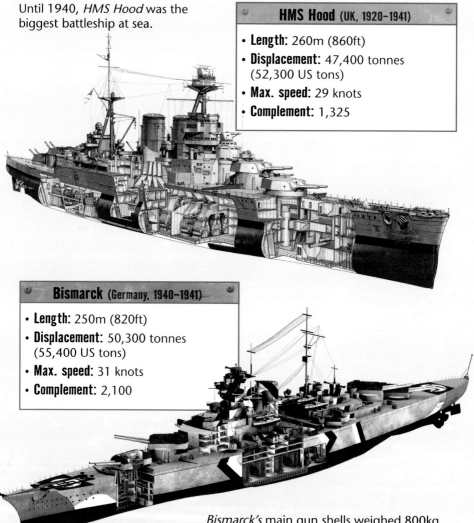

HMS Hood (UK, 1920–1941)

- **Length:** 260m (860ft)
- **Displacement:** 47,400 tonnes (52,300 US tons)
- **Max. speed:** 29 knots
- **Complement:** 1,325

Bismarck (Germany, 1940–1941)

- **Length:** 250m (820ft)
- **Displacement:** 50,300 tonnes (55,400 US tons)
- **Max. speed:** 31 knots
- **Complement:** 2,100

Bismarck's main gun shells weighed 800kg (1,760lbs). They sounded like a jet plane as they streaked down onto their target.

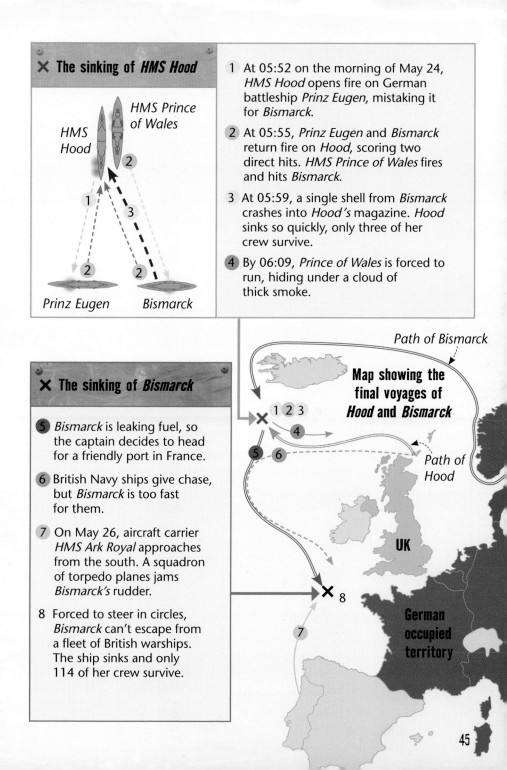

✕ The sinking of *HMS Hood*

1. At 05:52 on the morning of May 24, *HMS Hood* opens fire on German battleship *Prinz Eugen*, mistaking it for *Bismarck*.

2. At 05:55, *Prinz Eugen* and *Bismarck* return fire on *Hood*, scoring two direct hits. *HMS Prince of Wales* fires and hits *Bismarck*.

3. At 05:59, a single shell from *Bismarck* crashes into *Hood's* magazine. *Hood* sinks so quickly, only three of her crew survive.

4. By 06:09, *Prince of Wales* is forced to run, hiding under a cloud of thick smoke.

HMS Prince of Wales

HMS Hood

Prinz Eugen

Bismarck

✕ The sinking of *Bismarck*

5. *Bismarck* is leaking fuel, so the captain decides to head for a friendly port in France.

6. British Navy ships give chase, but *Bismarck* is too fast for them.

7. On May 26, aircraft carrier *HMS Ark Royal* approaches from the south. A squadron of torpedo planes jams *Bismarck's* rudder.

8. Forced to steer in circles, *Bismarck* can't escape from a fleet of British warships. The ship sinks and only 114 of her crew survive.

Path of Bismarck

Map showing the final voyages of *Hood* and *Bismarck*

Path of Hood

UK

German occupied territory

Rise of the carriers

Naval warfare changed forever after a surprise raid on Pearl Harbor, Hawaii, in December 1941. The damage done by the Japanese Navy to the US Pacific fleet showed that even the strongest battleships were vulnerable to aircraft carrier attack.

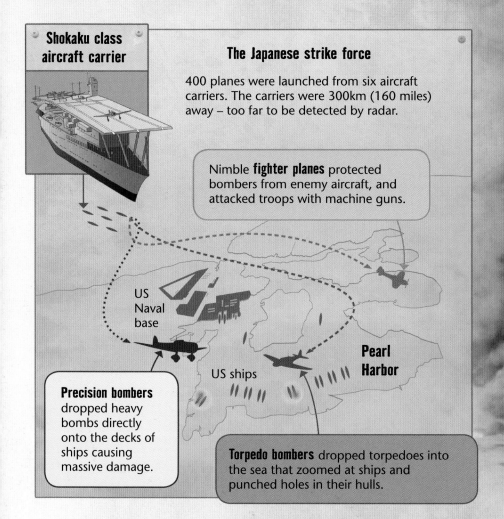

Shokaku class aircraft carrier

The Japanese strike force

400 planes were launched from six aircraft carriers. The carriers were 300km (160 miles) away – too far to be detected by radar.

Nimble **fighter planes** protected bombers from enemy aircraft, and attacked troops with machine guns.

US Naval base

Pearl Harbor

US ships

Precision bombers dropped heavy bombs directly onto the decks of ships causing massive damage.

Torpedo bombers dropped torpedoes into the sea that zoomed at ships and punched holes in their hulls.

Smoke billows from the battleship *USS West Virginia*. The ship sank after seven torpedo hits.

By the end of the raid, Japanese planes had sunk four battleships, destroyed hundreds of aircraft and killed more than 2,400 people.

River raiders

One of the quickest ships of the War was the motor torpedo boat, or patrol boat. These boats hugged the coast and made high-speed attacks and quick exits, often at night.

Higgins PT-71 (USA, 1942-1945)

- **Length:** 24m (78ft)
- **Max. speed:** 40 knots
- **Complement:** 17

Patrol boats have a 'planing' hull. The hull lifts out of the water and skims across the surface at high speeds – but can be damaged by rough seas.

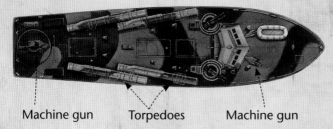

Machine gun   Torpedoes   Machine gun

The first patrol boats had to get close to their targets – 1km (0.6 miles) or less – before launching torpedoes.

Modern fast attack craft, such as the Special Operations Craft – Riverine (SOC-R), are often used to take special forces up rivers.

The SOC-R carries two machine guns, two grenade launchers and two mini-guns.

The craft and crew are covered in splinter camouflage. This makes them hard to spot against riverbank vegetation.

A day to remember

On June 6, 1944, the nations at war with Germany launched the largest amphibious invasion ever attempted – the D-Day landings.

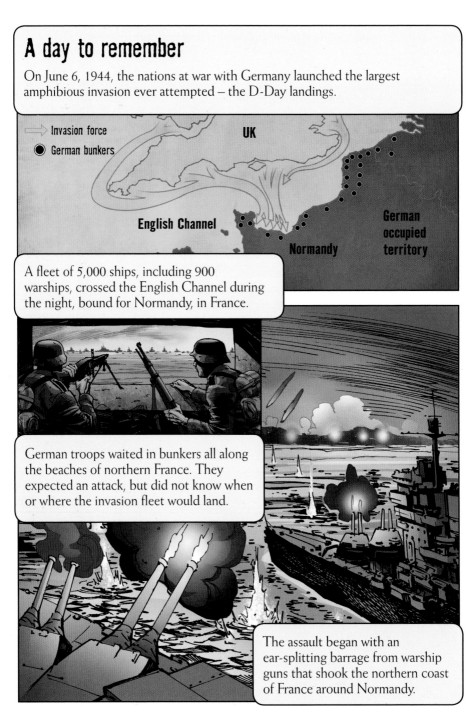

Invasion force

German bunkers

UK

English Channel

German occupied territory

Normandy

A fleet of 5,000 ships, including 900 warships, crossed the English Channel during the night, bound for Normandy, in France.

German troops waited in bunkers all along the beaches of northern France. They expected an attack, but did not know when or where the invasion fleet would land.

The assault began with an ear-splitting barrage from warship guns that shook the northern coast of France around Normandy.

More than 150,000 soldiers came over on all types of ships, including some fishing boats.

Soldiers scrambled down nets from transport ships to small landing craft, to take them onto the beaches at Normandy.

Big landing craft brought tanks and other vehicles straight to the fight.

High-speed torpedo boats escorted the landing craft to shore.

Thousands of brave soldiers fought their way off the landing craft under heavy German fire. By nightfall, the beaches were secured. In just one amazing day, the invading forces crashed into France and began the advance to Germany.

Last of the battleships

The battleship *Yamato* was the largest battleship ever launched, built to represent the might of the Japanese Navy. But Yamato sank no major warships and was blown to pieces in April 1945 by a fleet of American carriers. Navies stopped building new battleships.

Yamato battleship (Japan, 1941–1945)

- **Length:** 263m (863ft)
- **Displacement:** 73,200 tonnes (80,600 US tons)
- **Max. speed:** 27 knots
- **Complement:** 2,800

End of the line

American Iowa class battleships remained in limited service after the War ended. They were last used to launch missiles on land targets during the Gulf War of 1991.

Yamato's nine main guns had an incredible range of 40km (25 miles). Each three-gun turret weighed more than a destroyer.

The *Yamato* is shown here after being hit by a bomb during the battle of Leyte Gulf, near the Philippines, in 1944.

Iowa class battleship (USA, 1943–1992)

- **Length:** 271m (890ft)
- **Displacement:** 52,800 tonnes (58,200 US tons)
- **Max. speed:** 35 knots
- **Complement:** 2,700

The US Navy still maintains one Iowa class ship so it can be used in an emergency.

Going nuclear

From the 1950s, a new energy source was used for some warships, especially submarines – nuclear reactors. Ships with nuclear-powered engines don't need to refuel often, and so can make very long patrols.

A nuclear-powered ship needs to refuel after around 20 years of continuous use.

Nimitz class aircraft carrier
(USA, 1975–present)

- **Length:** 330m (1,090ft)
- **Displacement:** 106,300 tonnes (117,200 US tons)
- **Max. speed:** at least 30 knots
- **Complement:** 3,200 + 2,480 air crew

Nuclear-powered Nimitz class carriers are the largest warships in the world.

Kirov class battlecruiser
(Russia, 1980–present)

- **Length:** 250m (830ft)
- **Displacement:** 28,000 tonnes (30,900 US tons)
- **Max. speed:** 32 knots
- **Complement:** 710

After the largest aircraft carriers, Kirov class battlecruisers are the largest warships at sea.

Hidden hunters

Ultra-stealthy nuclear subs can undertake six-month patrols, often staying deep below the surface the entire time.

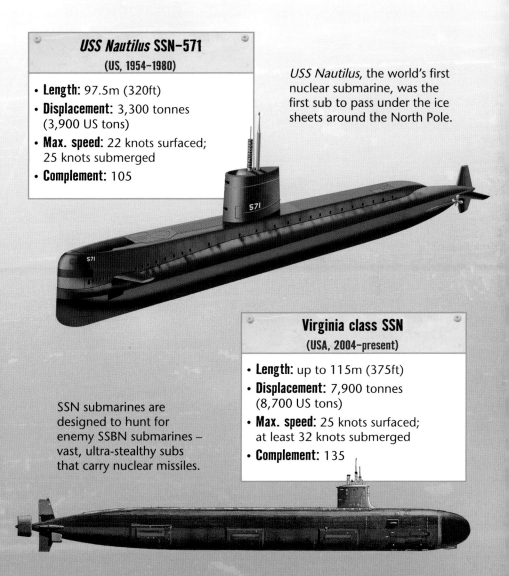

USS Nautilus SSN-571
(US, 1954–1980)

- **Length:** 97.5m (320ft)
- **Displacement:** 3,300 tonnes (3,900 US tons)
- **Max. speed:** 22 knots surfaced; 25 knots submerged
- **Complement:** 105

USS Nautilus, the world's first nuclear submarine, was the first sub to pass under the ice sheets around the North Pole.

Virginia class SSN
(USA, 2004–present)

- **Length:** up to 115m (375ft)
- **Displacement:** 7,900 tonnes (8,700 US tons)
- **Max. speed:** 25 knots surfaced; at least 32 knots submerged
- **Complement:** 135

SSN submarines are designed to hunt for enemy SSBN submarines – vast, ultra-stealthy subs that carry nuclear missiles.

Long-range lookouts

Radar is at the heart of every warship's navigation and weapons systems.

How radar works

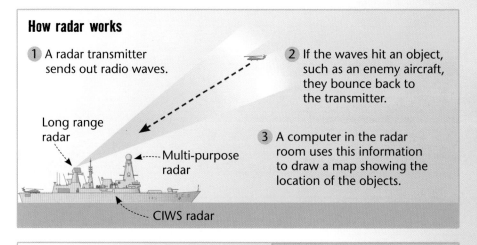

1. A radar transmitter sends out radio waves.

2. If the waves hit an object, such as an enemy aircraft, they bounce back to the transmitter.

3. A computer in the radar room uses this information to draw a map showing the location of the objects.

Long range radar

Multi-purpose radar

CIWS radar

Close-In Weapons System (CIWS)

Modern warships hold automatic radar guns known as CIWS. The guns defend against missiles up to 4km (2.5 miles) away.

Missile

Missile

1. The search radar finds two incoming missiles.

The CIWS gun can fire over 50 shells per second.

Search radar

Tracking radar

2. The tracking radar follows both missiles. Computers automatically aim and fire the gun at each target.

Radar arrays on top of the two main masts of this Type 45 destroyer can track hundreds of targets up to 400km (250 miles) away.

Lookouts keep watch from the ship's bridge, a vital job especially in close combat.

Built for stealth

Most ships are easy to spot on the open sea, but modern warships can disguise their exact position using disruptive paint schemes. Small warships, such as fast attack boats, can hide near the coast under camouflage netting.

Since ancient times, smoke has been used to conceal attacks. Here, two small assault craft have come from the large assault craft in the background. They are laying down a smoke screen...

...so that landing craft can follow them to shore under cover.

Invisible corvettes

Modern corvettes, such as the Visby class, are designed specifically for stealth.

Sloping surfaces deflect radio waves, so they don't bounce back to an enemy radar station.

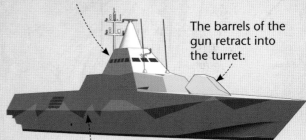

The barrels of the gun retract into the turret.

Disruptive pattern camouflage breaks up the lines of a ship against the sea.

Visby class corvette
(Sweden, 2009–present)

- **Length:** 73m (240ft)
- **Displacement:** 640 tonnes (700 US tons)
- **Max. speed:** at least 35 knots
- **Complement:** 43

Stealth features

- Exhaust gases are cooled to help conceal the ship from heat detectors.
- Special paint on the hull and superstructure can absorb some radar waves.
- The ship is powered by quiet water jets (see page 71).
- Weapons, including missiles and torpedoes, are hidden inside the superstructure.

Amphibians attack!

Large amphibious assault ships carry aircraft in hangars, and small landing craft in a well deck. The well deck can be flooded so the landing craft can sail straight out.

Launch platforms on an amphibious assault ship

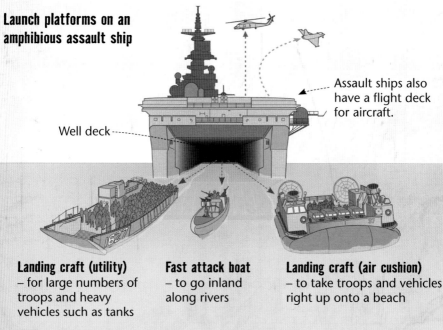

Assault ships also have a flight deck for aircraft.

Well deck

Landing craft (utility) – for large numbers of troops and heavy vehicles such as tanks

Fast attack boat – to go inland along rivers

Landing craft (air cushion) – to take troops and vehicles right up onto a beach

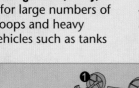

Landing Craft (air cushion)

❶ Fan propellers
❷ Exhaust vent for engine
❸ Bridge
❹ Jeeps
❺ Bow ramp
❻ Air cushion

LCAC (USA, 1986–present)

- **Length:** 26m (88ft)
- **Displacement:** 185 tonnes (200 US tons)
- **Max. speed:** at least 70 knots
- **Complement:** 5 crew + 180 troops

Air-cushioned landing craft can travel onto and across beaches.

Warships of the future

Over the next decade, a new generation of warships will patrol the oceans. These artist's impressions show how they might look.

M80 Stiletto
(US, began trials in 2006)

- **Length:** 27m (88ft)
- **Displacement:** 60 tonnes (66 US tons)
- **Max. speed:** 51 knots
- **Complement:** 3 crew + 12 troops

Designed for shallow water missions, the *Stiletto* speeds along on a cushion of air under its hull.

The *Stiletto* will be used to transport special forces along coasts and up rivers.

A ramp at the stern will let the Type 26 launch small combat ships into the water.

Type 26 global combat ship
(UK, planned for 2020)

- **Length:** 145m (475ft)
- **Displacement:** 5,500 tonnes (6,000 US tons)
- **Max. speed:** at least 28 knots
- **Complement:** 130

UXV combatant
(UK, planned for 2020)

- **Length:** 150m (500ft)
- **Displacement:** 8,100 tonnes (9,000 US tons)
- **Max. speed:** at least 27 knots
- **Complement:** 60

With its landing decks for helicopters, jet fighters and unmanned drone aircraft, the UXV will be a powerful, floating air base.

Zumwalt class destroyer
(US, planned for 2015)

- **Length:** 180m (600ft)
- **Displacement:** 14,800 tonnes (16,300 US tons)
- **Max. speed:** at least 30 knots
- **Complement:** 31

The Zumwalt's chief task will be to support ground attacks.

The main guns will be able to fire guided shells up to 160km (100 miles) away.

The ship's hull will fit up to 80 launch tubes for missiles.

World class carriers

The British Royal Navy is building two aircraft carriers in a new class, named Queen Elizabeth. Each enormous ship will carry up to 50 of the world's most sophisticated jet fighters and helicopters.

Queen Elizabeth aircraft carrier
(UK, planned for launch in 2020)

- **Length:** 280m (920ft)
- **Displacement:** 65,600 tonnes (72,400 US tons)
- **Speed:** at least 25 knots
- **Complement:** 600 ship's crew + 600 air crew

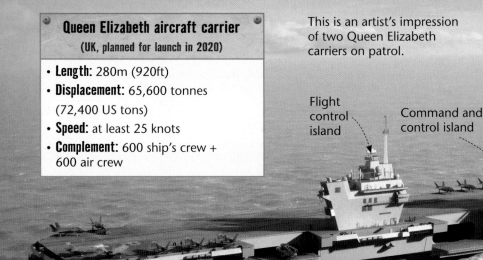

This is an artist's impression of two Queen Elizabeth carriers on patrol.

Flight control island

Command and control island

Proposed aircraft on board

- **F–35 Lightning II** (currently under development) A multirole fighter plane, used for anti-aircraft combat and to attack ground targets

- **AW159 Lynx Wildcat** (currently under development) An attack helicopter, used for anti-surface warfare, and search and rescue missions)

- **AW101 Merlin** A transport/utility helicopter, used to move troops and heavy equipment

Ramp, known as a ski-jump, to help planes launch without using a catapult track

Two enormous elevators will lift aircraft to the flight deck, each carrying two jet fighters at a time.

Inside the Queen Elizabeth class

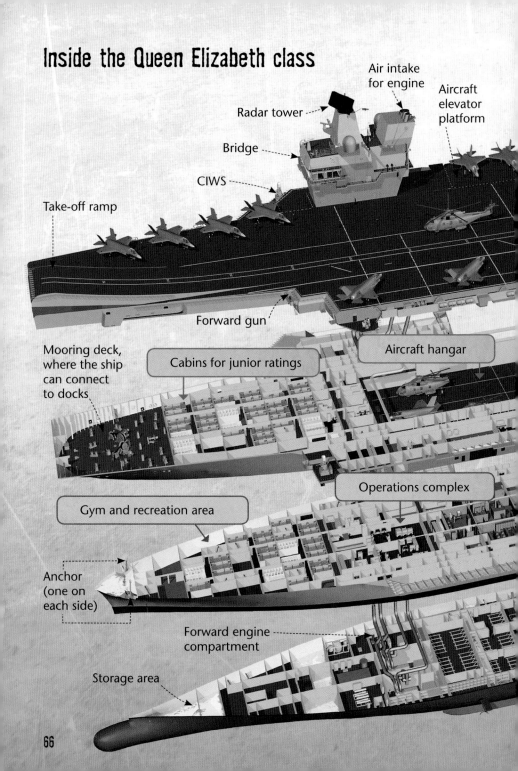

Air intake for engine

Radar tower

Aircraft elevator platform

Bridge

CIWS

Take-off ramp

Forward gun

Mooring deck, where the ship can connect to docks

Cabins for junior ratings

Aircraft hangar

Operations complex

Gym and recreation area

Anchor (one on each side)

Forward engine compartment

Storage area

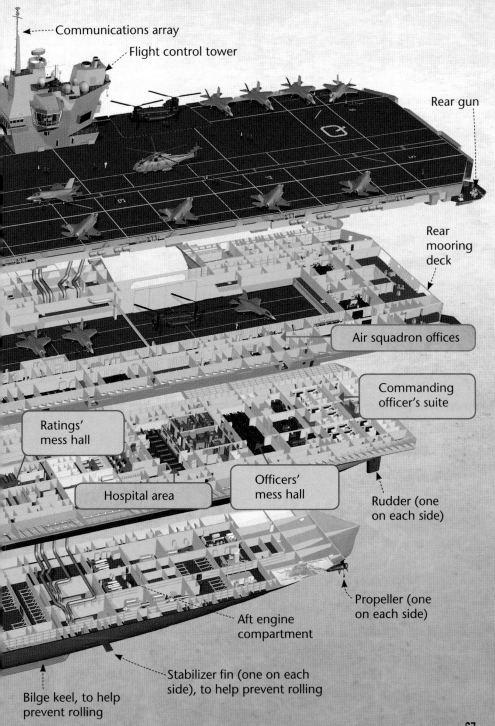

Communications array

Flight control tower

Rear gun

Rear mooring deck

Air squadron offices

Commanding officer's suite

Ratings' mess hall

Hospital area

Officers' mess hall

Rudder (one on each side)

Aft engine compartment

Propeller (one on each side)

Stabilizer fin (one on each side), to help prevent rolling

Bilge keel, to help prevent rolling

Building a warship

It takes years to design, build, launch
and test a warship before it is ready
for active duty.

Sections of the hull of a new
Queen Elizabeth class aircraft
carrier are brought together
in an assembly yard in
Glasgow, in Scotland.

1221

How warships are assembled

- The hull and internal decks are built in sections, often in different shipyards.
- Finished sections are bolted and welded together in an assembly yard.
- The ship is launched into deep water and towed to a dry dock, where the masts and equipment can be added.
- When the work is complete, the dock is flooded and the ship sails away for trials, to check that it's ready for active service.

Staying afloat

Ships float by pushing away, or displacing, an amount of water greater than their own weight. A force known as *buoyancy* lifts the ship up.

The weight of a warship is often described as its *displacement*, or the amount of water it pushes away.

How buoyancy works

Gravity pulls the boat down.

Sea level

Water displaced by the ship pushes away from it.

Buoyancy created by the displaced water pushes the ship up.

Steering

Changing the angle of the rudder at the stern makes the ship turn to starboard (right) or to port (left).

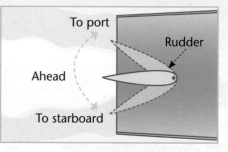

To port

Rudder

Ahead

To starboard

Moving forward

Since the end of the age of wind and sail, warships have used engines turning propellers to push them through the water.

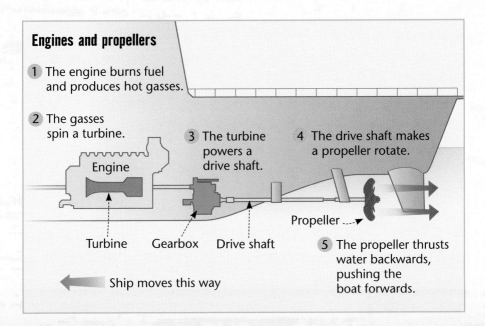

Engines and propellers

1 The engine burns fuel and produces hot gasses.

2 The gasses spin a turbine.

3 The turbine powers a drive shaft.

4 The drive shaft makes a propeller rotate.

Engine

Turbine   Gearbox   Drive shaft

Propeller

Ship moves this way

5 The propeller thrusts water backwards, pushing the boat forwards.

Jet boats

Lighter ships can use their engines to power jets that push water out of the stern.

This prototype jet ski, called Blackfish, uses jets to speed around coastlines.

Water jets are faster and work more quietly than propellers. They also function in very shallow water.

Ship-to-ship

Thousands of miles from any friendly port, supply ships transfer food and fuel to warships on the move.

Guide line

Fuel hose

Flight control tower of the *USS George Washington*, an aircraft carrier

Cylinders to store life boats

Crates full of dry supplies, such as food and ammunition, are winched across a set of cables.

This combat support ship (right) sends fuel and supplies across to an aircraft carrier (left) in the Persian Gulf. This is known as underway replenishment.

Warships on the internet

For links to websites where you can find out more about warships, from ancient triremes to the latest nuclear submarines, go to the Usborne Quicklinks Website at **www.usborne-quicklinks.com** and enter the keyword **warships**.

A diver explores the wreck of a Russian Koni class frigate at the bottom of the Caribbean Sea near the island Cayman Brac.

Glossary

This glossary explains some of the words used in this book. If a word is written in *italic* type, it has an entry of its own.

AMM Anti-missile missile, used to destroy incoming missiles.

amphibious assault An attack on land launched from water.

ASM Anti-ship missile, used to attack enemy ships.

barrage A gunnery attack by more than one warship.

battleship A heavily protected warship designed for gun battles with the most powerful enemy ships.

beam The width of a ship at its widest point.

bow The front part of a ship.

bridge The observation and command room of a ship.

broadside All the guns from one side of a ship firing at the same time.

bulkhead Thick, watertight walls inside the *hull*.

buoyancy The force that pushes a ship up, making it float.

CIWS Close-in Weapons System. A gun that acts as a last line of protection against incoming enemy targets.

cog A tough, single-sail warship, with fighting platforms at the bow and stern. Mainly used from 1200-1400.

convoy A group of merchant ships protected by navy *escorts*.

corvette A light and fast warship used in coastal waters.

cruiser A multi-purpose warship smaller than a *battleship* and larger than a *destroyer*.

dazzle camouflage Bright patterns of lines and shapes painted onto ships to confuse enemy gunners and submarines.

deck A floor or level platform on or within a ship.

destroyer The largest multi-purpose warship in common use today.

dreadnought A powerful type of *battleship* taking its name from *HMS Dreadnought*, the best battleship of its day.

drone An unmanned, remote-control military vehicle, ship or aircraft.

escorts Warships used to defend merchant ships from attack.

frigate A multi-purpose warship, slightly smaller than a *destroyer*.

galleon A warship with several masts and sails and ranks of guns along each side of its *hull*. Mainly used from 1400-1750.

galley (room on a ship) Where the food is prepared and served on a ship.

galley (ship) An ancient type of warship powered by ranks of oarsmen.

hangar The storage and maintenance space for aircraft.

helmsman A sailor who steers the ship.

hull The main body of a ship.

ironclad A steam-powered warship made of wood but covered in iron. Mainly used in the mid 19th-century.

keel A tough wooden spine running the length of a ship's *hull*.

knot (kt) Speed at sea is measured in knots. 1kt = 1.8km/h (1.2mph).

LAM Land attack missile, used to attack targets on land.

LCAC Landing craft air cushion. An amphibious transport ship that rides on an inflatable cushion of air.

littoral combat Fighting close to a coastline or river inlet.

missile A rocket-propelled explosive device.

operations room The main fighting and communications area in a ship.

planing hull A ship's *hull* designed to lift out of the water and skim across the surface at high speeds.

port The left side of a ship.

radar Technology that uses radio waves to locate and track objects.

raking fire Shooting cannonballs through the *stern* or *bow* of an enemy ship.

ram An underwater metal spike at the *bow*, used as a weapon on ancient *galleys*.

ratings Junior sailors who serve in a Navy and report to officers.

rudder A flat piece of wood or metal at the *stern* of a ship, that turns to change a ship's direction.

salvo Firing multiple *shells* or *missiles* at the same time.

SAM Surface-to-air missile, used to attack flying targets.

shell An explosive canister fired from a gun.

ship-of-the-line A type of warship designed to sail in a long line. Mainly used from 1750-1850.

sonar Underwater listening and detection equipment.

starboard The right side of a ship.

stern The rear part of a ship.

superstructure The parts of a ship above the *hull*.

torpedo An underwater *missile*.

trireme An ancient, wooden *galley* with three ranks of oarsmen.

turret A metal dome or covering that protects a ship's guns and gunners. Turrets can rotate so that guns can fire in most directions.

well deck A flooded area at the *stern* of a ship, where small boats can dock and launch.

Index

Page numbers marked with an 'a' are found underneath the flap on that page.

Acknowledgements

Every effort has been made to trace and acknowledge ownership of copyright. If any rights have been omitted, the publishers offer to rectify this in any future editions following notification. The publishers are grateful to the following individuals and organizations for permission to reproduce material on the following pages: (t=top, b=bottom, r=right, l=left)

cover Battleships ©Purestock; **p1** *USS Yorktown* hit by Japanese bombers in July 1942 ©Bettmann/Corbis; **p2-3** ©Purestock; **p6-7** ©Purestock; **p8-9** courtesy of Defenseimagery.mil; **p10-11** ©Peter Russell Photography; **p10a-11a** ©Crown Copyright/MOD. Reproduced with the permission of the Controller of Her Majesty's Stationery Office **p12** courtesy of Defenseimagery.mil and Photographer's Mate 3rd Class Andrew King, US Navy; **p14** Courtesy of BAE Systems **p15** all ©Adrian Dean/F1ARTWORK; **p18-19** courtesy of Defenseimagery.mil and Mass Communication Specialist 3rd Class Nathan Parde, U.S. Navy; **p20-21** ©AgustaWestland; **p23** (tr) ©Adrian Dean/F1ARTWORK **p24** (b) ©Adrian Dean/F1ARTWORK; **p25** Tony Bryan, *Spanish Galleon 1530–1690* © Osprey Publishing; **p26-27** ©Adrian Dean/F1ARTWORK; **p30** (t) Tony Bryan *Union Monitor 1861–65* ©Osprey Publishing; (b) ©buyenlarge / Getty Images; **p32-33** ©Hulton Archive/Stringer/Getty Images; **p35** ©Underwood & Amp Underwood/National Geographic Society/Corbis **p36** (t) Paul Wright *German Battleships 1914–18 (2)* ©Osprey Publishing; (b) ©ArtTech/Aerospace Publishing; **p37** (b) ©Imperial War Museum SP2200; **p40-41** (t) Tony Bryan *US Navy Aircraft Carriers 1922–45* ©Osprey Publishing; (br) Ian Palmer *German Destroyers 1939–45* ©Osprey Publishing; **p42** Ian Palmer *German Pocket Battleships 1939–45* ©Osprey Publishing; **p44** (t) Tony Bryan *British Battlecruisers 1939–45* ©Osprey Publishing (b) Ian Palmer *German Battleships 1939–45* ©Osprey Publishing; **p46-47** ©Library of Congress/digital version by Science Faction/Getty images; **p48-49** Courtesy US Navy SEALs www.seals.swcc.com; **p52-53** ©Corbis; **p53** (b) Peter Bull *US Fast Battleships 1938–91* ©Osprey Publishing; **p54** (t) ©ArtTech/Aerospace Publishing; (b) ©Adrian Dean/F1ARTWORK; **p55** (b) Tony Bryan *US Nuclear Submarines: the fast-attack* ©Osprey Publishing; **p57** courtesy of BAE Systems; **p58** courtesy of Defenseimagery.mil and Mass Communication Specialist 1st Class Michael Moriatis, U.S. Navy; **p59** ©Adrian Dean/F1ARTWORK; **p61** courtesy of Defenseimagery.mil and Mass Communication Specialist 2nd Class Kristopher Wilson, US Navy; **p62-63** all ©Adrian Dean/F1ARTWORK; **p64-65** courtesy of BAE Systems; Lynx helicopter ©Agusta Westland; **p66-67** ©Crown Copyright/MOD. Reproduced with the permission of the Controller of Her Majesty's Stationery Office; **p68-69** courtesy of BAE Systems; **p71** (b) courtesy of QinetiQ North America; **p72** courtesy of Defenseimagery.mil and Photographer's Mate Airman Janice Kreischer, US Navy; **p74-75** ©Julian Calverley / Corbis.

Use of photos from Defenseimagery.mil does not imply or constitute U.S. Department of Defense endorsement.

Additional illustrations by Giovanni Paulli, John Fox, Zoe Wray and Helen Edmonds
Series editor: Jane Chisholm   Series designer: Zoe Wray
Digital design by John Russell   Picture research by Ruth King
With thanks to Captain Bob